PARENT SURVIVAL TRAINING

A Guide for Parents of Teenagers

PAUL A. SMYTH, Ph.D.
JANET BENNER, Ph.D.

Second Edition

Joelle Publishing, Inc., Santa Barbara, California

PARENT SURVIVAL TRAINING
A Guide for Parents of Teenagers

Published by:
Joelle Publishing, Inc.
P.O. Box 91229
Santa Barbara, CA 93190-1229

DESIGN BY WORDS & DEEDS, INC.

Printed in the United States of America

Library of Congress Catalog Card Number 87-082072

ISBN 0-942723-13-9

To our children

ACKNOWLEDGMENTS

Much goes into the making of a book. We would like to acknowledge and thank those who assisted in making this one.

The very talented and creative staff of Parent Survival Training: Karen Hickman, Kate Murphy, Kathy Kane, Betty Chase, Katherine Larsen and Mae Karam contributed greatly to the book. The staff of Klein Bottle lent administrative support.

Linda Mears was our able editor. Suzette Mahr of Words & Deeds did the book design and computer work. Robert Howard designed the cover. The book was printed by BookCrafters.

Thousands of courageous parents participated in the Parent Survival Training workshops and gave generously of their ideas and insights. To these, special thanks and much love. Their gift will be appreciated by other people in need of assistance in the difficult task of parenting teenagers.

And to our own three beauties, Ken, Andy, and Rachel who suffered through our parenting blunders only to turn out so well and to make us very proud, we give thanks.

CONTENTS

	Preface	vii
	Epigraph	ix
1	Introduction	10
2	The Training	20
3	The Problem	28
4	Vicious Circles (Maintaining the Problem)	50
5	Minimum Goals	62
6	Strategies — Monkey Wrenches	70
7	Roadblocks	82
8	Resources	92
	Comments from Parents	105
	Appendix	107
	Index	124
	About the Authors	126

PREFACE

This book was developed for parents with the assistance of the many people who attended "Parent Survival Training" (PST) workshops. The workshops focused on how parents could improve their home situations and hopefully, relieve some of the stress and pain they were feeling.

Parent Survival Training was designed for parents because even though they often do not realize it, parents have the maturity, flexibility, motivation, and creativity to solve problems; attributes which are often lacking in their children. The hope is that this book will give you a sense of your own flexibility and creativity in dealing with your family.

One of the greatest benefits of the workshops was the camaraderie, the coming together with people in like circumstances who shared willingly of their experience and support. It is a wonderful feeling to discover that we are not alone, and that, in fact, there is someone whose circumstance may be even more difficult than our own. It is fun to have a laugh at our shortcomings and the ridiculous situations we get into with our children. While the book is unable to retrieve that "community" feeling, you may get a sense of it by reading some of the comments and responses from parents included in the book.

Please be aware that there are no "RIGHT" answers nor are there "MAGICAL" solutions to problems. What works for one family of a 16 year old runaway may not (and probably won't) work for another family with a 16 year old runaway. Solutions are as varied and numerous as are the families themselves. So keep in mind as you make your way through the book that the solutions you seek are unique and special to you and your family.

Since the "ANSWER" is not to be found here, what can this book offer?

This book offers techniques and strategies for closely looking at your own particular situation and experimenting with possible solutions. We call it *unpacking the problem*. Simply stated, *unpacking* is looking at a problem, component by component, step by step, to make the solution easier to find. You will find in the Appendix a cut out sheet entitled "Unpacking Problems" which lists the major steps of the process. Tear out this sheet and pin it on a wall or on your mirror for those times when you need a quick review.

Hopefully some of these strategies will benefit you and your situation as they benefited the many parents who attended workshops.

If they don't work for you, at least you will have tried one more thing, and you will know more about what doesn't work!

The Teacher

If he is indeed wise he does not bid you enter the house of his wisdom, but rather leads you to the threshold of your own mind.

—Kahlil Gibran

1 INTRODUCTION

Parent Survival Training (PST) was, in the mid-1980's, a government funded series of workshops and seminars designed to educate parents in ways to solve the difficulties they were having with their teenagers. The classes showed parents methods of UNPACKING any problem: taking it apart aspect by aspect, and arriving at solutions that met the unique needs of the different families. The *Parent Survival Training* book was created as a result of these classes.

Most professionals approach parenting education by embracing the idea that parents need **information**. For example, if the child has a drug problem, the parents need information about drugs to solve the child's problem. If there is a problem with truancy, the parent then needs information about why children do not go to school.

Many parents have also taken this "informational" approach. They believe that what is required in problem solving is more **information**. Therefore, they seek out **experts** to give them answers. They look for "The Answer" which they can plug into their problem, and that will solve it. Typically, as parents search for the answers to these problems, the problems become more elusive, more frustrating and consequently, a vicious circle of non-problem solving occurs.

The information parents receive is conflicting. They must do this, or they should do that. Marijuana causes this — pills may cause that — not attending school will result in such and such. If the child runs away, this will surely happen. Information about sex and relationships is conflicting and confusing. Often the sought after information reveals more about hypothetical *cause and effect* than about solution. (See Traits of Families of Deliquent Youth in Appendix.)

There are several (not just two) sides to most issues and parents will usually be able to find as much evidence to support one view as another. It eventually becomes clear that the informational approach holds no one answer that will facilitate a solution to the problem.

Parent Survival Training (PST) has taken a different approach. This unique method focuses on the **process of solving problems**. It is based on the premise that parents can learn, through practice, to solve their own problems. PST addresses itself to the blocks that are in the way when people approach a problem and the reasons why the problem continues. PST helps people in attacking any family conflict and discovering the elements involved in problem solution.

This new approach requires an open mind, some new thinking, and often a new perspective.

Consider this for example: most of the time problems consist of repeated behavior. If a behavior only occurs once, it is not defined as a problem. The problem *is* the repetition of the behavior. The problem not only involves the repetition of the child's behavior but also the repetition of the parents' attempted solution. The continuing lack of resolution creates the recognition that a problem exists. If a young person comes home late once, it is not a problem. If he continually misses deadlines the resulting distress and attempts of the parents to change the child's late behavior add the catalyst that leads to defining "coming home late" as a problem. Complicating things, the young person will deny that a problem exists or that he has a problem. He may even insist that his parents are the problem. And he may be right. Usually the parents are actively involved in the conflict before the behavior is defined as a problem.

Remember Rubic's Cube? Let's think about it for a moment. The Cube is not a problem until one starts to participate in finding a solution. It is not a real problem until many solutions do not work. Obviously one approaches the puzzle in the best way he knows to reach solution. And he works and works while frustration builds. At different stages, different approaches to the Cube are required. The problem must continually be redefined before solution can be reached. The problem solver must change his perspective often to different views which are not what he might typically expect.

Most parents when dealing with their problem teenagers do not redefine the problem but continue with their initial definition. If, with Rubic's Cube, the approach remains along the same lines for some time, the puzzle is manipulated to no avail and frustration builds. Likewise, with the parent-teenager conflict, if the problem is approached and manipulated in the same ways week after week, the frustration level becomes tremendous. The lack of creative thinking, the inability to change, to redefine and start over again is common. Parents often find themselves stuck.

Parent Survival Training helps to get parents **unstuck**. It teaches ways to "unpack" a problem—to take the problem apart. This requires redefining and breaking the problem down into its smaller elements. The PST method has been very effective with thousands of parents who took the classes and risked doing the exercises outlined in this book. Training begins when and at whatever point the parent needs it and facilitates the redefining of problems and the structuring of strategies for resolutions.

What are these "problems" as defined by parents? In the several years that PST conducted it's classes, parents were asked what they viewed as their main problem. What would be your guess at the most common response?

Parents overwhelmingly named "communication" and "respect" as the main problems they experienced with their teenaged children. What do you suppose happened to drugs, truancy, theft, and promiscuity? From parents of delinquents and non-delinquents alike, the overwhelming answer to "what is the biggest problem" was communication and respect. The problems of theft, etc., were mentioned down the list along with wrong friends, tardiness, runaway, and so forth.

If a problem is defined as "communication" it can easily be seen that no quick solution will be forthcoming. Communication is so general a concept that it involves a myriad of specific behaviors. This problem cannot be solved and defining it as **the** problem keeps it elusive. When this is pointed out to parents and when they are asked to be more specific they then move to another area that is equally general and unsolvable. They continue to redefine the problem in general ways. Helping parents learn to define problems specifically, by specific behaviors, was the major task in the work of PST with families in conflict.

PST created a method that aids parents in defining a problem in concrete terms. The concrete behavior that is the problem has to be defined for a number of reasons. Most importantly, young people can deal with and understand specific behaviors better than abstract concepts. Parents can better deal with concrete problems because they can measure the results, define their goals (what they wish to change), and are better able to recognize a solution when it occurs. It is clear that "communication" cannot be measured qualitatively nor quantitatively so it is not obvious when or if "communication" has occurred. Therefore, communication is too ambiguous to define as a problem and resolution is impossible to determine. PST helps parents to avoid seeking solutions to unsolvable and ill defined problems.

In its work with parents, PST also inquired into what methods parents had used in solving the problems they experienced with their teenaged children. (A list of these methods can be found in the Appendix.) We have already mentioned the very popular "information" approach. The list is long and has many ideas which seem constructive and beneficial. People tried professional counseling, talking with their children, logic, examples, yelling, nagging, praying, physical violence, bribes, and restrictions.

Usually parents who came to training expected to learn a new strategy. Yet when their usual methods are examined it is discovered that there is nothing wrong with these ploys (with the exception of physical violence which is cyclical and damaging to everyone).

Parents already have the solutions and they know the answers. What they don't know is how to use them effectively. They nag in the wrong way. They bribe in the wrong ways. Their timing is off. They have no technique in their logic to make it functional. The "packaging" of their solutions is very poor. Few adults would accept the type of discussions that parents try with teenagers because usually they are wrought with prejudice, anger, frustration, non-listening, and are not very interesting. Unfortunately, the teenager has heard it all time and time again. A particular food may be beneficial and taste good, but if you eat it night after night you will quickly tire of it. Variety must occur in these discussions with children, a disarming little attention getting something.

Again, parents know all the methods of dealing with their problem teenager. They simply have to learn to "package" them more effectively, make them become alive and functional. Individual parents have different talents in this "repacking." Individuality is a key issue. PST teaches parents how to capitalize on their talents. Parents need to learn to recognize their personal strengths and weaknesses so to enhance their flexibility. In this way they will improve their approaches and techniques in dealing with their family conflicts. They will discover that some of their old answers are functional but need only to be redesigned and repackaged. Then "communication" with their 14 year old son or daughter can be improved. Perhaps the problem of "communication" can be resolved after all if redefined and described in concrete terms.

The experience of PST was that parents want to be successful in their parenting. They want to do the right thing. This sincere desire makes them very educable. Parents have lots of information and lots of personal resources but because of preconceived notions, continual frustrations, and because of slipping relationships with their children they cease to demonstrate creativity.

There were parents in the PST groups who had great ability when organizing the use of people-power in solving problems at work. There were people who organized volunteer clubs or organized fund raisers, who put on socials, who solved problems at the plant, who made executive decisions everyday. They were people influencers. They assisted other employees in solving problems about coming to work on time, about improving efficiency and communication on the job, and all manner of other issues that were potentially difficult.

When these same people returned home after their daily activities they were not able to solve problems at all. One business executive/ parent stated,

"The only one who'll listen to me at home is the dog."

And that parent spent a lot of time with the dog! At work he supervised 10 people and did a good job of it. When the class examined some of his methods, how he approached these people, what reward systems he used, and how he solved problems, they found he demonstrated a remarkable amount of creativity, imagination, and enthusiasm. When he returned home, he showed very little enthusiasm or creativity. If he had done the same things at work that he did at home he wouldn't have lasted long as a supervisor.

On the job, we would never get away with the methods we use at home to solve our domestic problems. We would be embarrassed about these tactics.

Parents typically discipline their kids, argue with their kids, and have discussions with their kids without another adult nearby because they sense how foolish their arguments sound. Parents begin these discussions with many attitudes and feelings including frustration, demand for power, being right and uncompromising. These attitudes must be rerouted and repackaged if we expect to achieve successful solutions to family problems. Parent Survival Training is a method of "repacking" problem solving in the family.

To summarize, Parent Survival Training will be a different experience for most parents. Initially, it might be frustrating because PST is a new way of approaching problems and a new way of discovering solutions. Do not expect the ideas and methods herein to come easy. They will require practice.

This book is asking parents to try some things that are strange, unfamiliar, and at times uncomfortable. Don't shy away from the frustration and lack of initial enthusiasm but take the risks and proceed with the book. Especially keep your sense of humor. It is guaranteed that you will have some fun and insight will be forthcoming.

NOTES TO MYSELF

2 THE TRAINING

TRAINING: *developing or forming habits, thoughts, or behavior by discipline and instruction.*

Now consider yourself in training. This training is unusual and may at times go against what you believe to be so. At PST we discovered that the best, most effective training came with *doing* rather than *telling*. We could proceed from here with still further telling but we know that would be of little benefit to those of you who are struggling in crisis with your children.

So this is training by doing. With that in mind, here is how to best accomplish your training.

In the chapters that follow, interspersed with the text, there are three kinds of activities for you to do; exercises, homework, and as part of the homework, role-play. There are also some rules which we call "Axioms" that will help keep you focused.

EXERCISE

As you read each section, complete the exercises by jotting down your answers in the space provided. You may wish to date your answers to see if they are different six months from now. Use the pages titled NOTES TO MYSELF for further jottings, dates, events, whatever. The book is designed to build on each step of new information, so complete each step before going to the next. Doing each exercise will actually make everything clearer and the process more effective. Keep in mind that we are working for results not just more information. The results will come from doing.

Each of the following chapters also includes a homework section delineated by:

■ HOMEWORK

These assignments will provide you with opportunities to practice some of the ideas. You must practice any new skill before you can master it. You can read about tennis, watch people play tennis, and talk to tennis players about the game, but you will never really understand until you play yourself and you'll never really be good at it unless you practice. So practice. Do the Homework! Try some things and see what happens.

ROLE-PLAY

Role-play, a way to practice new skills, is a powerful tool to help you see, hear, and feel what goes on in your home. An ideal role-playing situation is to have two friends help you, so one can observe. Often the role-players are so involved that it is difficult to objectively look at what is happening. So find some friends and practice, practice, practice.

When the directions say to role-play, the circumstances will be carefully described. You will need to decide who will play the role of the parent and who will play the role of the child. Switch roles often to get a feel for the difference. It is important to stick to the role and stay in character, especially if you are playing the child.

Try to be like the kids really are, not like you would like them to be. (Assuming that if your kids were always polite, cooperative, and sensitive to your feelings you wouldn't be reading this book.)

At first role-play is not an easy thing. You will feel some embarrassment, some shyness, a lot of resistance but all this will pass and you will find this activity can actually be fun. Many parents have said this was the most difficult aspect of the course and the most necessary and valuable. We want to emphasize that at first role-play can be difficult to get into, but it is one of the most important and useful aspects of your training. Try a little by yourself, in private, to get over the initial shyness about it. Watch yourself in the mirror. You'll get used to the idea and soon will be comfortable about it. Then do it with your friends. Practice.

Axioms

The dictionary says axiom is a self-evident truth. Obviously our truths are not self-evident or this training would not be necessary. We prefer the definition from logic or mathematics: *a proposition which is assumed without proof for the sake of studying the consequences that follow from it.*

We want you to consider the Axioms as rules to follow when dealing with your children. These rules can help keep you from doing the same things time and again, the same things you've always done, the things that end in vicious circles.

What Do You Tell the Kids About Parent Survival Training?

One of the questions that always came up in the workshops was, "What do we tell the children about what we are doing?"

Should the parents hide the book and not tell the kids anything, or should the parents openly discuss the process they are involved in with their children. It is an interesting question. The best advice is probably to be open. Simply leave the book lying on the coffee table and don't mention it. Some of the best things happened to parents when their children approached them to pursue problem solution à la PST after the children discovered the book lying about. Some even role-played each other.

It is important that you feel free to enter the process being honest with yourselves. If there are things that you wish to record that you don't want your children to know, then put the book away in a private place. You can still discuss the book and maybe later will feel more free to share it with them. You know your kids; this will have to be a judgment call. This must be considered *your thing*—something you're doing for yourself. You don't want to hinder your ability to participate fully in the process.

Okay, now you're ready to begin! Follow along and step by step you will learn to "unpack" your problems. Relax, have some fun and realize there's hope.

GOOD LUCK!

NOTES TO MYSELF

NOTES TO MYSELF

3 THE PROBLEM

PROBLEM: *1) an intricate unsettled question. 2) a source of perplexity or vexation. See* Mystery.

That is how Webster defines a problem. Defining *The Problem* is often very difficult, a source of perplexity! As parents we tend to believe the problem is quite clear. Yet when asking family members, "What is the problem?" there are mixed answers.

Mama might say:	The problem is that the garbage is not getting taken out.
Teenager might say:	The problem is that Mom is always on my case about the garbage.
Papa might say:	The problem is that our kid doesn't respect authority.

When asking a teenager what his problem is, as so often happens in counseling, the reply would likely be:

"Hey, man, I don't have a problem. It's my mom (dad, parents) who has the problem."

For the purposes of these exercises let's define a problem as a circumstance or ongoing event that is causing someone pain (physical or emotional). Since you are the one doing or reading this book, we can assume you are that someone so we will work on the problem as YOU see it and attempt to alleviate some of that pain.

EXERCISE

List five problems that you're having with your teenager.

1. ____________________
2. ____________________
3. ____________________
4. ____________________
5. ____________________

On the following page is a list of 10 problem areas which were very frequently mentioned by parents. Rate these from one to 10 in order of importance for you and your family. Other family members may wish to do the same.

_____	Coming home on time	_____	Chores
_____	Drugs and alcohol	_____	Stealing
_____	Lying/dishonesty	_____	Discipline/punishments
_____	Respectfulness	_____	Family communication
_____	"Bad" friends	_____	School performance

The following table shows how other parents rated these issues. About 85 percent of the responses by parents fell into the following 10 problem areas. They are ranked according to frequency with number one, respectfulness, being the most frequently mentioned.

7	Coming home on time	3	Chores
9	Drugs	10	Stealing
5	Lying	6	Discipline/punishments
1	Respectfulness	3	Family communication
8	"Bad" friends	4	School performance

Axiom 1 **When parents and children are working on the same problem, the solution is easier to find.**

One way to begin working on the same problem is to make certain that everyone's perception of the problem is similar.

EXERCISE

Look at the picture of the woman on the opposite page.

How old is she?

How old does your spouse think she is?

Your child?

Other family members?

What did you discover about different perceptions of the same thing?

Any surprises?

You probably know by now that there are two ladies in the picture, an older one and a younger one. Ask someone to show you the one you cannot see. You will also find help in the Appendix.

AGAIN:

Axiom 1 **When parents and children are working on the same problem, the solution is easier to find.**

We often don't see things the same way as the other people in our families. It is not a question of right or wrong — simply of perspective, different points of view, different ways of seeing the same thing.

You know how easily an argument can happen when one person, your child for example, sees only the young woman and you see only the older woman. (Our gramma refused to believe there was a young woman in the picture.) Both people may be correct.

The most vigorous arguments and conflicts come when both parties are correct. Each believes he is right and the other is wrong. To break that conflict, one needs to get in the other's shoes to see from the other's position. Looking at and understanding the other's viewpoint provides the power and techniques to manipulate or teach the other something new. ***If you know how someone else sees things, you can more easily find methods to alter his view.***

You might attempt to see a problem as your child sees it. Try to understand his perspective. Then try to help your child to see the problem the way you see it. Show your child clearly what you mean (like you explained the different faces in the picture.)

The following homework assignment may help you and your family discover some of each other's perspectives.

■ HOMEWORK

1. Talk to your family. Organize a family meeting to ask what each person sees as the major problem in the house. The discussion should last 10 minutes or so. No coffee, no TV, no stereo. Just family. (You might wish to use the lady picture as an ice-breaker.) Be certain everyone has a chance to be heard, that everyone is allowed to participate. Don't let the grown-ups monopolize the meeting.

2. Next, talk to your teenager and find out what is THE most important thing in his life right now. (It probably isn't world events, inflation, taxes, or the stock market! But it's important to him!)

3. Now that you have a better idea of the different family members' problems and their different perspectives, try to choose one problem that you wish to attack.

Good! You've completed your homework. But — you had trouble choosing just ONE problem? Then please read on!

The following activities will assist you in choosing the problem you want to **attack**. (You will notice the frequent use of military terms;

attack, battle, tactics, etc. For some families it may be just a small skirmish, for others a full scale war!)

One way to begin focusing on ONE problem (battle) is to decide which ones we are losing and which ones we are winning.

EXERCISE

List battles (or problems) that you are currently winning and losing. The examples may not be right for you but are here to get you started.

Battles I'm/We're Winning *Example:* *She is at least going to school.*	Battles I'm/We're Losing *Example:* *She lives like a pig!*
1. ____________	1. ____________
2. ____________	2. ____________
3. ____________	3. ____________
4. ____________	4. ____________
5. ____________	5. ____________

For those things you have listed under "Winning Battles," give yourself gold stars, hurrahs, kudos, and congratulations. Is there one similarity in these? How did you get into the position of winning? Oddly, some things just seem to happen *automatically*. Parents often can't say how they got their child to use good table manners. It just happens that way. See if you can think through some of these winning battles. How did you win them? In any case, continue to do what you're doing because it must be working!

Looking at those things you listed under "Losing Battles," this may be the place to begin to select one problem to attack first. Carefully examine this column and **choose a problem that is both small and manageable. One that you have a chance to win.** For example, if you listed "drugs" as a battle you are losing, you can see that one is complicated and very tricky. Try to pick one that is less complex, like hanging up wet towels, or picking up dirty socks. You need to achieve some success and confidence before you confront those biggies.

Now, from the list of battles you are currently losing, you have selected a problem to work on. (Remember, it needs to be **small and manageable**.) Write down the problem here.

____

____

____

Axiom 2 **To attack a problem it must first be defined in clear, concrete, tangible, specific terms.**

Now we can look at one aspect of "unpacking" using the problem you have written down. To "unpack" a problem means to dismantle it into small, manageable components. Take the problem you listed above and begin to "unpack" it by defining it in the clearest, most specific behaviors you can think of that are associated with it.

For example: "My problem is that my kid doesn't respect me."

"Respect" here is a fairly broad and general word. What does "respect" look like? How will you **know** when you have solved (won) this problem and gained "respect"?

We might redefine this problem as: "My problem is I can't stop my kid from using foul language in front of me so I know he doesn't respect me."

You can see the difference.

While we still have the losing battles list in mind, consider the following.

Axiom 3 **It's time to give up losing battles.**

Are there problem areas that you and your teenager have been battling over for years which never seem to change? Consider giving them up! (See Giving Up Losing Battles in the Appendix.)

In fact, don't you have a parent who still reminds you (nags you) to use more light for reading, to stop chewing your nails or whatever? After 30 or 40 years he or she is still talking about it? Don't you wonder when they will give it up?

■ HOMEWORK

1. Pick a small battle such as the too long showers, the socks left in the living room, or the very loud stereo.

2. Set a time limit for yourself: one week, two days, or even an hour. During that time you **will not** mention or even hint at this battle. **Ignore it**! Give it up. (And guess what, he already knows how you feel about that one anyway.)

3. Try it. It can be very interesting. Write down any surprises.

Good! Wasn't that empowering?

Now let's take a look at another typical battle. This problem might be stated:

"My problem is my children don't clean their rooms when I tell them to. I will know my problem is solved when their rooms are cleaned."

What do you suppose is the difficulty with this problem statement? Okay, who defines CLEAN? What is clean to your children most certainly will not meet your criterion. CLEAN is not clear! In defining a problem attempt to discover exactly what the behavior is that is driving you crazy. Define the problem in terms of behaviors that you can see, touch, hear, etc.

For the room cleaning example, it might be better stated:

"My problem is he won't make his bed."

Bed making still leaves room for judgment calls but generally if the sheets aren't showing and there aren't too many lumps, the bed is considered made.

EXERCISE

*Rewrite the problem you selected to work on here. Make it clear, concise, and specific.**

____

____

____

**Would a five year old know exactly what you mean?*

And to keep in mind your successes, list again the areas you are not having problems in.

1. ______________________________________
2. ______________________________________
3. ______________________________________
4. ______________________________________
5. ______________________________________

When considering battles and wars, here is another concept to think about.

Axiom 4 **As parents and as people, we need to maintain a broad perspective on our lives and the lives of our children.**

It is a great tragedy for parents when we are so determined to win a particular battle that we end up losing the war.

For example, if we alienate our children over the issue of their messy rooms or friends we don't approve of, we may find they will shut us out of their later lives. Of course these issues are important, but let's be sure to examine the price of winning. It may be steeper than we wish to pay.

It's important to put our kids' behavior into perspective.

The figure on the next page shows a hypothetical view, a TIMELINE of one person's life over a 40 year span. It shows the frustrations and pain experienced by the parents of that person. We have all, or will, as parents faced some of the frustrations depicted here. Sometimes if we can view our difficulties from a distance our perspective of current events changes. At a distance, more events come into view and each seems smaller. Consider a postage stamp on a letter, then on a billboard. The TIMELINE is a graphic method of representing such a perspective.

Time Line

Figure shows a hypothetical view of the frequency of conflicts and frustrations parents have with their children over the first 40 years of the child's life.

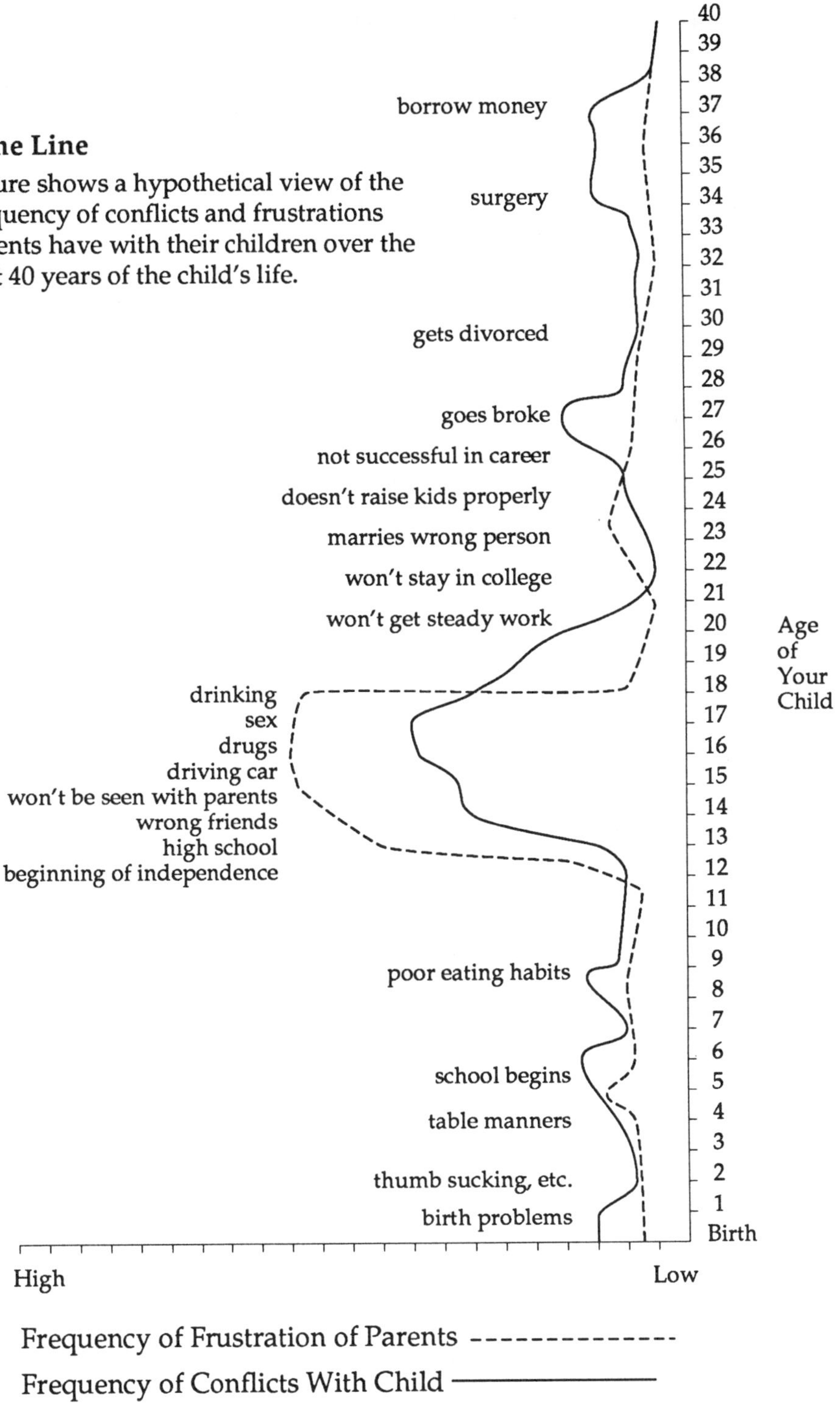

Remember that most of our children will live to be at least 40 years old. They do not die when they become 18, **they simply become legal adults.**

Looking at the early years in our figure, we can see that many events occur that could cause frustration (represented by the dotted line). These frustrations can cause conflict and disagreements with our children regarding their behavior (represented by the solid line). The conflict arises because of our frustration over the difference between our ideal expectations of how our child should act and his actual behavior.

The frustration seen here, as a result of the events, belongs to the parents exclusively. It can be controlled by us as parents. We are the ones who feel it, who manifest it. We bring it about; we own it. Sometimes parents don't see this. They think the child **causes** the frustration and that the child must change in order for it to go away. In fact, it is the expectations of the parents that create the level of frustration, not the actual events or behaviors of the child nor the resulting conflicts.

The figure shows various events that might occur in the lives of children which might cause concern for parents. Birth problems, school begins, poor eating habits, as examples, can cause conflict and frustration for parents. Please note the teenage years where the frustrations are shown to outweigh the conflicts, though both increase during these years.

During the children's teenage years, many parents feel the pressure of having just a little more time in which to raise the kids "properly." If the kids don't learn to clean their rooms now, they'll be "irresponsible" adults. It is also during these years that the child is attempting to establish some autonomy from his family. The resulting tug of war sometimes takes the form of rebelliousness on the part of the child. It is not an easy time for parent or child.

Now, note in the figure that the frustration drops off when the child reaches the age of 18. This is because when the child becomes 18 the parents define the conflicts and behaviors of their child differently. The child is then an "adult" and "out of the control" of the parents.

Parents make statements like,

"I have only 94 more days to suffer because he will be 18 and I can quit worrying."

This thinking works well because when the 94 days are up the parent finally puts the worry and frustration where it belongs, back on the child.

The argument is that if when the child reaches the magical age of 18, the parents can reduce their frustration, they should be able to reduce it when their child is 15 or 16. Actually, the reduction in frustration comes about mostly because the state of California liberates the parents of their responsibility when their children reach the age of 18. The age is different in different states. What if you lived in a state which liberated children at the age of 16.

Perhaps we should liberate ourselves and not wait for the state to do it. (At least emotionally.)

In any event, the hypothetical TIMELINE shows that other events in the later life of the child will occur and hopefully parents will be able to keep the extent of frustration below the amount of conflict. This is possible because as the child passes the age of 18, parents no longer *define* themselves as the ones who need to worry. They *define* their child as having the responsibility, thereby removing themselves from the suffering.

Perhaps all this discussion will help to put things into perspective for you. At least it took you away from struggling with the statement and formulation of the ONE problem that you were working on. Please state that chosen problem again here:

____

____

____

By now your problem is in still clearer focus; more specific and concrete.

Be careful. Watch out for changing the problem, perhaps in small ways. We sometimes fool ourselves by changing the problem just a little to avoid really confronting it. Or we might change it because we decide another is more important thereby avoiding trying to solve just one.

So, to begin to "unpack" any problem we must first put the problem into perspective, does it really need solving? Then the problem must be defined in small, manageable, specific terms. And care must be taken not to change the problem in ways that keep us from dealing with one issue at a time.

The next step in "unpacking" is to discover what we, the parents, may be doing to keep the problem going.

NOTES TO MYSELF

NOTES TO MYSELF

4

VICIOUS CIRCLES

(Maintaining The Problem)

VICIOUS CIRCLE : *a situation in which effort to solve one problem merely results in the creation of a new problem and in increased difficulty.*

(Webster again)

Whether we like to believe it or not, if a problem continues over time, we, the parents, are probably doing some things to keep the problem going. The next step in *unpacking* is to look at the ways in which we may be *maintaining* the problem.

How, exactly, does this relate to the problems you are having with your kids? Well, how often do discussions go around and around, tempers escalating in the process? For some parents it seems that no matter what they do or say, and in discussions on nearly every topic, they end up in a vicious circle and accomplish absolutely nothing that they set out to do.

Mama:	Please clean up your room.
Teenager:	Not ***this*** again. I'll do it later....
Mama:	That's what you've been saying for the last five days.
Teenager:	So, I've been busy. Don't bug me. You're always on my case.

And away they go! Sound familiar?

EXERCISE

Take a minute to think about a recent vicious circle you were caught in with your child. Write down what happened. Who said what? How did it get started? How did it end?

____

____

____

We all know what it's like to get hooked into one of those vicious circles. Right? And how does it happen? That's an excellent question and no one seems to have a clear answer. (Find another example of a vicious circle in the Appendix.)

Since we can't figure out how we got in, let's see what keeps us in there. Perhaps then we can gain some insight into how to get out.

Axiom 5 **"Maintainers" keep vicious circles going.**

Maintainers are the things we say, or do, or **believe** that keep vicious circles going. The vicious circles that hook us with our kids into the same old arguments. Some of the things we do during *losing* arguments actually maintain those arguments, keep them going.

One way to stop the vicious circle is to identify our **maintainers** and replace them with behaviors that will help rather than hinder the process of solving problems.

Some examples of **maintainers** are:

1. Always having to have the last word.
2. Bringing up unrelated wrongs the child has committed.
3. Always being "right."
4. Nagging.
5. Getting argumentative.
6. Asking questions we know the answers to.
7. Continuing to talk, talk, talk, telling the child what he already knows.
8. Yes… but!

(Find more **maintainers** in the Appendix.)

EXERCISE

*List three of your most common **maintainers**.*

1. ________________________________

2. ________________________________

3. ________________________________

What is your child's best line to push your button (i.e. to make you angry)? Write it here.

____

It just gets you every time, doesn't it?

Speaking of time... **timing** is another issue that always plays a part in maintaining problems and <u>vicious circles</u>. You hear about comedians and the timing of their jokes? Timing has to do with rhythm and appropriateness of the event, action, or discussion. You know that in adult relationships you are careful about the receptivity of the other person to your requests, complaints, and so on. Think of this as it relates to approaching your children about problems.

Write down the place and time where you usually end up in a fight with your child. Example: "In the kitchen, in the morning as I'm leaving for work."

____

____

Okay, you're doing great!

There is another aspect of this **maintainers** phenomenon that is helpful to examine.

MYTHS!

MYTH defined: a traditional story of unknown authorship... serving usually to explain... the origin of man, or the customs, institutions, or religious rites of a people.

MYTHS are those things we have come to believe about parents and kids and parenting itself. MYTHS may be guiding our reaction to our children's behavior and our view of ourselves as parents. Your beliefs, the MYTHS you believe to be true, can most certainly be **maintainers** in those <u>vicious circles</u>.

Axiom 6 — **Check your MYTHS (beliefs) for those which are no longer operative.**

The following is a list of MYTHS, some which you may hold to be true. (Also see MYTHS in the Appendix.)

1. Broken homes cause delinquency.
2. Girls are less trouble than boys.
3. Parents are responsible for the behavior of their kids.
4. Kids who get good grades don't get into trouble.
5. If the kids are bad the parents were bad.
6. Educated adults make the best parents.
7. Good parents meet all their kids needs.
8. Good parents never yell.
9. Alcohol is not as bad as dope.
10. If you do all of the normal things (zoo, picnics, ball games) your kids will be good.
11. If it was good enough for me then it's good enough for you.

EXERCISE

Circle the MYTHS *which you believe. What are your other* MYTHS*? Write them down.*

1. ____

2. ____

3. ____

So, in examining MYTHS we discover that some actually may be true, some not so true. Probably MYTHS are at the base of our behavior and, in fact, ***we are currently acting off the MYTHS held to be true by* our *parents.***

You may decide that some MYTHS you call beliefs, some you will refer to as facts. You may believe, for example, that "Good parents never yell", or that "Girls are easier than boys." Nonetheless, we prefer to call all such popularly held beliefs MYTHS because we have found none to be universal or always true. Give a little on yours. Look at them closely. Try to determine if the ones you steadfastly believe really deserve all that loyalty.

Now that you have finished answering all the preceding questions, you should start to understand your **maintainers** as well as the elements of the vicious circle. It's time for homework again. This should be fun!

HOMEWORK

Now we're going to role-play. First you may want to review role-playing in Chapter 2. Get together with your spouse or a friend or two. Explain role-play to them.

One of you will play the "parent," the other gets to be the "kid." Create a vicious circle (getting nowhere fast) where one of you wants one thing and the other wants the opposite. (Example: You want her to do the breakfast dishes. She wants to go to the beach, now!) Let it go on for awhile so you can really **feel** it. After a few minutes, switch roles, so you can feel what it's like to be the kid, too. (Some people find it so freeing!)

To bring things really into focus, jot down what happened in the spaces below.

Who won?

____

What was the problem? Did the problem change somewhere along the way?

____

____

Did you discover some **maintainers**? What were they? For example, did you as the parent keep it going by having to have the last word? Or did you say "yes, but" to every point the child made. As the child did you push all the parent's buttons just to see how that feels?

"Parent's" **maintainers**

____

"Kid's" **maintainers**

____

Comments

____

____

How did it feel to be the "kid"?

____

____

How did it feel to be the "parent"?

____

____

Such an experience, huh? Good. You get an A!

To *unpack* a problem (besides letting some problems go) and define it in concrete terms, we must also be aware of the **maintainers** we use that keep the problem (and vicious circles) going.

And always, as we go, remember that we as parents must continue to reassess, redefine, reexamine. What am I doing? What is he doing? Is this issue really important to me? Remember that in solving Rubic's Cube, you must continually reassess, change your perspective, be on your toes. Always use your energy to refocus the issues, not to **maintain** them. Eventually, you will get what you want. And we're certain that what you want will be best for your teenager, too.

Next we'll move on to some other ideas about getting out of those vicious circles.

NOTES TO MYSELF

5

MINIMUM GOALS

GOAL: *the result or achievement toward which effort is directed.*

MINIMUM: *the least quantity allowable.*

You are anxious to begin solving those problems you listed in Chapter 3. You have also zeroed in on one concrete problem to work on. And you have looked at **maintainers** that keep the problems going. Here is the next step in *unpacking* a problem.

Axiom 5 **Limit your goals.**

When parents are asked to state a goal for various issues with their teenager their reply might be:

"I want my child to be a responsible person."

This appears to be a reasonable goal, doesn't it? But what exactly, does it mean? How will the parent know when the goal has been achieved? What must the teenager do to satisfy his parents' goal? What does being responsible mean?

When probed further, we find parents will modify their goals to things like:

"Getting home on time."

"Not taking things that don't belong to him."

"Keeping his room neat and clean."

That's better. Each of these behaviors represents a demonstration of responsible behavior. Each of these goals is somewhat more clear. Still, we need to break them down even further to a ***minimum goal.***

A ***minimum goal**** is:

1. **Specific**; when, where, how much, how often.
2. **Attainable**; a key word if you are looking for success.
3. **Realistic**; for both you and your teenager.
4. The **smallest** behavior you are willing to accept.

   *These are just to get practice in winning. It is not the final goal.

The following is an example of a problem with a ***minimum goal.***

Problem:	My son is not going to school.
Goal:	I want him to go to college.
Minimum goal:	I want him to attend **one** class each day for **one** week.

"What?" you say. "How can I ever live with that? I'm giving up all my values as a parent. My kid must be in school all day every day!"

Of course, but how is he going to get to college if he's not going to school **at all**? Let's be realistic. We're looking for a starting place. A goal we can hope to achieve. So the goal has to be limited! Get the idea?

Now, let's practice setting ***limited goals***.

EXERCISE

Write down the problem you have been working on. (Remember, in concrete terms.)

____

____

*Pick a **minimum goal** for the problem:*

Is your goal realistic?

____

Is it attainable?

____

Super! If you answered YES to the last two questions, and have a concrete, measurable statement for the goal, you are on the right track.

Now, practice setting ***minimum goal*** for pretend problems. Practice is important to success!

Here comes another Axiom. Still more to think about!

Axiom 8

Kids should suffer the consequences of their behavior.

Remember this statement when you begin setting up goals. If you set a goal that is going to put you in the position of having to "suffer" along with your kid to achieve it, think twice about it. This is a common mistake parents make when they set up restrictions for their kids. For example,

Parent to child: "I got a call from school today. They said your grades are so bad you're on the verge of flunking out. So, for the rest of this quarter, I'll have to stay home with you every night to make sure you do your homework."

Who is going to suffer in this one? Look at the same situation where the teenager will be suffering the consequences of his own behavior instead of the parent.

Parent to child: "I got a call from school today. They said your grades are so bad you're on the verge of flunking out. Looks like you'll need to talk to your counselor and teachers to find out what you have to do to stay in school. Please bring me a note from them saying you've done it."

You can see the difference!

Or how about,

Parent to child: "I got a call from school today. They said your grades are so bad you're on the verge of flunking out. Looks like you may want to see the vocational counselor for some job training information. Hope everything works out!"

With these tips in mind for setting up ***minimum goals***, move on to some homework, more work on *unpacking* a problem.

You are an excellent student!

■ HOMEWORK

Find your role-play partner again and begin by creating a vicious circle. You remember how. This time, though, the "parent" should have a ***minimum goal*** in mind before he begins. Try it out and see how it works.

You can record what happened on the next page.

What was the problem being discussed in the vicious circle?

____

____

What was the "parent's" ***minimum goal***?

____

Was the goal realistic?

____

Did the "kid" go for it?

____

Comments:

____

____

Good! Excellent! Isn't this fun?

You've mastered three steps of *unpacking* a problem. You have defined your problem in concrete behaviors. You know what you've done in the past to **maintain** the problem. And now you have a ***minimum goal*** in mind; what you will settle for as a solution to your problem.

Don't forget that if the typical teenager has his way, he will argue so the problem and goals keep changing. He will keep you angry and confused, increasing your use of maintainers and muddying the water. Hold your ground! Pick your problem, your time and place, and your ***minimum goal***. Do not be manipulated into doing and saying things you do not choose to do and say. DO NOT BE MOVED!

Even though we have considered a great deal of information, you are still stuck in that vicious circle! The final step in *unpacking* the problem will provide you with strategies to break the vicious circles so the other three steps have a chance work.

On, then, to **Strategies**.

STRATEGIES – MONKEY WRENCHES

STRATEGEM: *1) an artifice or trick in war for deceiving or outwitting the enemy. 2) cleverly contrived trick or scheme for gaining an end. See Tactic.*

(Webster again)

Rather than see Tactic, see "Monkey Wrench."

Monkey Wrench is our term for tactics or strategies you as parents can use to stop the vicious circles — to muck up the works. The purpose: to get your child's attention.

Another word for Monkey Wrench might be intervention; directed, particular, calculated actions which interrupt and stop the vicious circles, the behavior systems we have set up with our children.

Many PST parents claimed the Monkey Wrench idea was the most fun and interesting part of *unpacking* the problem. For many, it will be the first enjoyable, visible, and hopeful sign that they have some power and control over events within their families.

Monkey Wrenches do not in themselves solve anything. What they do is stop the circles, reduce the viciousness, and provide an opening so a ***minimum goal*** can be achieved.

A WORD OF CAUTION: be sure to have your ***minimum goal*** well planned in advance of applying a Monkey Wrench. It would be a shame to gain your kid's attention (and stop the vicious circle) and not have anything else to say. So practice developing your ***minimum goals***.

Following is a list of Monkey Wrenches other parents have come up with. Using your creativity and imagination you can think of hundreds more. Select actions that are comfortable for you, or even uncomfortable for you at first. Anything, anything can be a Monkey Wrench if it catches your child off guard and breaks the pattern of the vicious circle.

SOME MONKEY WRENCHES

1. **Change the subject** — just begin talking aimlessly about something else totally unrelated to the issue at hand.
2. **Silence** — this gets them everytime. Just stop talking. Mid-sentence would be especially good.
3. **Honesty** — say exactly how you feel about the issue.
4. **Give in** — agree or say your kid is right.
5. **Walk away** — leave the fray. Just go into the next room. Again, mid-sentence might be quite effective.
6. **Change the place** — if you always have the messy bedroom discussion in the messy bedroom, take the discussion to the front porch, the car or whatever.
7. **Go to the extreme** — if your child won't take out the garbage, take the garbage bags to his room and leave them there.
8. **Compromise** — give in to a point that will really surprise them, give half way. You know what compromise means, you do it with adults all the time. Think of negotiations and contracts.

9. **Contracts** — used to clearly define what your expectations are of your child. "Okay, Joey, if you're willing to make your bed each day for one week there will be a $5.00 bill waiting for you on your pillow on Sunday. Let's write it down and we'll both sign the agreement. It will be our contract."
10. **Humor** — begin to make jokes about the situation. "Look what we're doing, like two old crows fussing at each other." Put on a smile and come up with a laugh or two.
11. **"I" statements** — "I feel very helpless." (Quite disarming, huh?) Or, "I feel so confused, I don't know what's best for either of us." (That would be hard for the parent to say. But the kid would certainly notice it.)
12. **Touch** — as you are making your big point (for the 17th time?) reach over and touch your child on the shoulder or on the hand. You might be very surprised at your child's response to this. Touch may just be THE most effective Monkey Wrench.
13. **Paradox** — whatever your child would ordinarily expect you to do, do the opposite. Make it spectacular. Example: "Look, Joey, I don't want you to even think of coming home until 2:00 am. So that's that!" Or, "Since you didn't pick up your clothes yesterday as I asked, perhaps you should leave them on the floor for another day or two."
14. **Do what your child always says you do, what he accuses you of.** — Example: he says, "You're always yelling at me." You begin to really shout, continuing with the same line of conversation.

15. **Change the time** — if the battle usually begins in the morning, intentionally begin it in the evening after dinner. Pick your own time. But do not participate at the usual time a vicious circle begins.

You will find more Monkey Wrenches in the Appendix along with examples from parents who have used these techniques.

An Axiom related to the use of Monkey Wrenches.

Axiom 8 **Don't do what you've always done.**

Change your tactics. Do something different. Remember **maintainers**, those things you always did that kept the problem going. If you always shout, try silence or walking away. If you always fight in the living room at dinner time, start a fight in the bathroom when you usually have breakfast. Try something new. Break those circles. Be imaginative, stand on your head right in the middle of the discussion. Be creative. Don't just act by habit. Actively take charge of your behavior. You can do it!!

EXERCISE

Pick a Monkey Wrench.

Now, armed with your Monkey Wrench, go back to the step-by-step process of unpacking *your problem.*

Plan your strategy.

My problem *in concrete terms is:*

____

____

My **maintainers**, *what has kept me in* vicious circles *in the past:*

____

My ***minimum goal*** *is:*

____

My Monkey Wrench *is*

____

And here we go to Homework.

■ HOMEWORK

1. Role-play again. Do the role-play with your friend, who by now is quite expert at it. Let the vicious circle begin. Then try your Monkey Wrench. The one you decided on in the Exercises. See what happens.

   Ask your friend how it felt. Was your friend surprised?

2. Find two Monkey Wrenches that work and two that don't. Be sure to go through all four steps: Problem, **maintainers,** ***minimum goal,*** Monkey Wrench. (Remember that the effective Monkey Wrench comes out of defining the Problem, knowing the **maintainers**, and having a ***minimum goal***!)

   Monkey Wrenches that work!

1. ______________________________

2. ______________________________

   Monkey Wrenches that don't work!

1. ______________________________

2. ______________________________

See how much fun this can be! By now you and your friend are probably laughing. And, again, how empowering! You can see how Monkey Wrenches can disarm your opponent giving you control over the situation.

Bit by bit you can begin, now, to employ some of these strategies in the discussions you have with your children.

If it seems that what you tried was ineffective, go back to planning and regroup. Try something still different. There are no failures. Each experience gives you more information about what not to do, and brings you closer to success. Try something else. As we pointed out, there are hundreds of potential Monkey Wrenches.

As a reminder of your new approach, cut out the Monkey Wrench sheet on the following page and pin it to the wall next to the sheet on *Unpacking Problems*. These should be somewhere that is your private place, maybe in your closet or your own bathroom; somewhere where you can glance at them often to reinforce your new tools. And as you discover newer, more effective Monkey Wrenches, add them to your pinned up list.

NOTES TO MYSELF

MONKEY WRENCHES

Cut out and post in your house

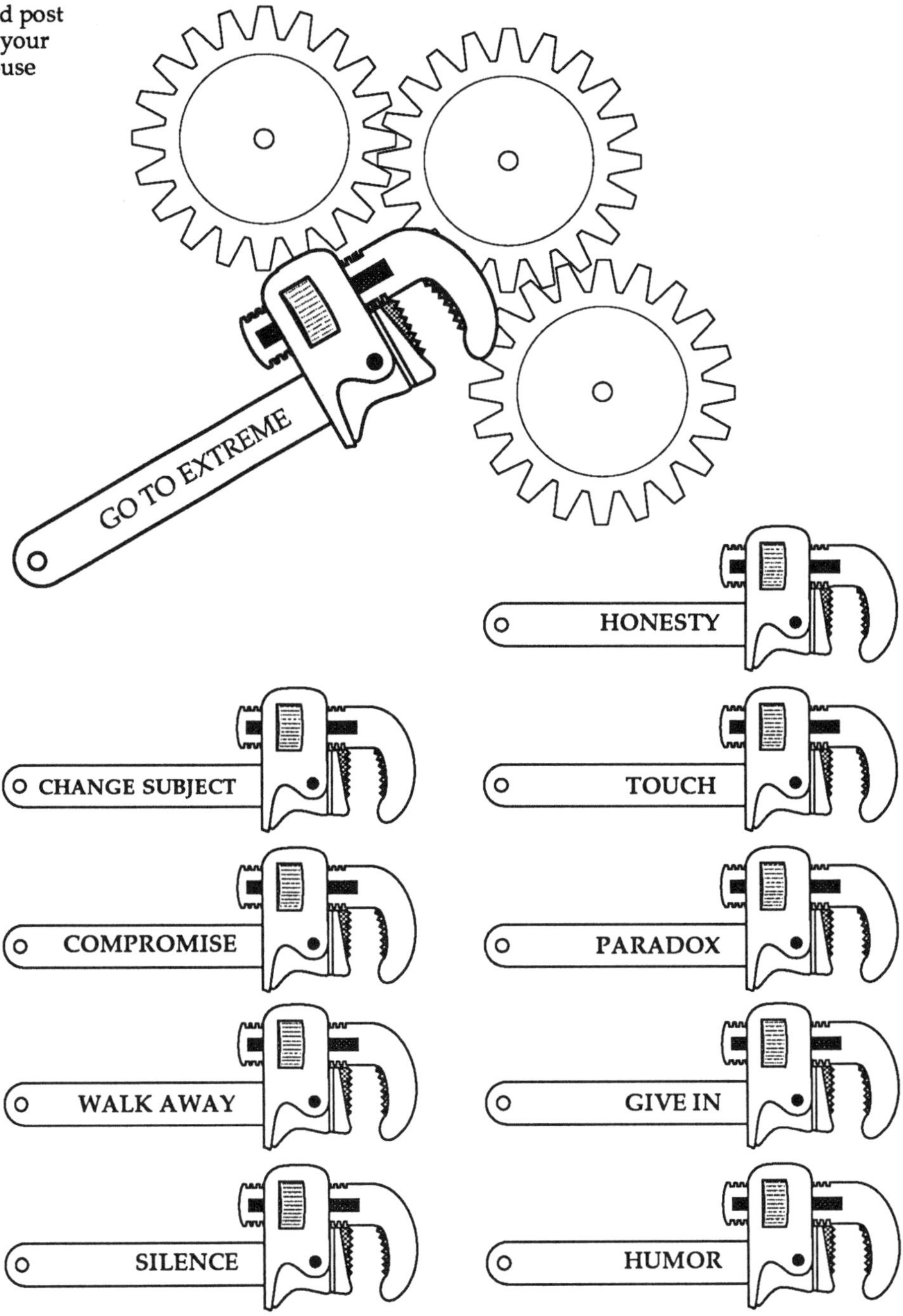

NOTES TO MYSELF

7
ROADBLOCKS

ROADBLOCK: *an action, condition, etc. that obstructs progress toward an objective.*

You now have a sample list of strategies to help break those vicious circles. The next part is up to you and is probably one of the hardest. That is... actually trying some of these things. Doing it. Giving it a whirl. Going for it. The really difficult part of all this is getting past ourselves so the process has a chance to work.

We are our own blocks to changing; it's scary and it's unknown.

PST's definition of Roadblocks is: *those things which keep us from changing or doing something different.*

One way to help yourself 'get out of your own way' is to examine the things you tell yourself about the problem. These statements comprise part of the Roadblocks and by articulating them they are out in the open so you have a better chance of finding ways around them.

So, let's attempt to uncover some of our Roadblocks.

EXERCISE

List three reasons why this training and these strategies won't work and why this book is worthless.

Example: It'll never work with my *kid.*

1. ______________________________

2. ______________________________

3. ______________________________

By acknowledging and saying these things out loud, you become more aware of some of the Roadblocks to solving your problems with your teenager.

For the majority of people a gigantic learned and enculturated list of *shoulds* and *should nots* stands in the way of participating freely in these activities. These are the MYTHS of our culture, the values of our parents and grandparents.

Times change. We, as parents have to be changeable and adaptable to keep up. The world is smaller and much faster paced than it was in the years when we were children. We cannot expect our parents' values then to apply to our children now, 30 or 40 years later.

Consider, for example, the notion (the Roadblock):

"They (my children) should do as I ask without my having to do all this."

Who says they "should"? Did you accept freely and completely what your parents asked of you without question? Will an intelligent person ever do that for anyone? Your teenaged children should have the right to expect explanations and some justification for what is requested of them.

Consider another example:

"I'm afraid I'll look silly."

Of course *looking silly* really means *seeming vulnerable or weak.* Men, especially in our culture, are taught not to appear vulnerable nor silly. Actually, that's what's so great about Monkey Wrenches. They are exactly what your children don't expect of you and that really gets their attention.

Another Roadblock frequently mentioned by people in the PST classes was "fear of failing." You already feel you are failing, in some way, or you wouldn't be reading this book and participating in this training. You need to believe that no attempt at new solutions is a failure. None. Each thing you try gives you new knowledge, new insight. Most attempts will give you another perspective and you will probably learn something new about your child.

EXERCISE

List some things that are comfortable about not *changing.*

____

____

And thus, more Roadblocks. (See others' Roadblocks To Monkey Wrenches and Ways To Overcome Roadblocks in the Appendix.)

Now list three ways to overcome your reluctance... your Roadblocks.

____

____

____

Good!

And we like the one that goes:

"It's more okay if I choose to be silly rather than having my kid always make me feel that way."

Perhaps the key to all this is that ***you do make the decisions about how you will act, how it will go, what the outcome will be.*** Trying out these new things can empower you in ways you had forgotten possible when relating to your family.

The Roadblocks that keep you from doing it are only ideas. You impart to them their reality. Consider the quotation:

> People are disturbed not by things
> But by the views which they take of them.
> —Epictetus, 1st Century A.D.

In this book we have not mentioned love. The nearly unconditional love of parent to child is the purest love we know. Depend on this love, call it forth when you are having an especially tough time. Remember that this is your child whom you have cared for all these years, he is not an alien, someone from outer space. He or she may act awful, may disappoint you, will probably bring you hurt but remember you can use the tools in this training with love to regain the equilibrium that you both need to feel comfortable. It may take a form that is unfamiliar to you, but it can be right and it can be workable.

Stretch yourself, be willing to take some risks. Have some fun. Bring some joy to a situation that at times seems bleak. Try something new. Remember your love several times each day. Let it replace the resentment and anger you have felt so often, if for no other reason than love works better than resentment. More creative solutions come from love than from anger and hate.

Maybe a Monkey Wrench for you will be to let it go. Just go sit under a tree for a month. Whew! What a relief! Whatever, do it with gusto, do it with courage, do it with love. You can, you know.

And let's return once more to the ways to *unpack* your problems.

1. Select a Problem; define it in concrete terms.

2. Check yourself closely to see what you're doing to **maintain** the problem—to keep those vicious circles going.

3. Set some ***minimum goals*** that you could consider acceptable solutions to the Problem.

4. Use Monkey Wrenches—strategies to change the pattern of your interactions with your children.

5. Now check the Roadblocks that might be keeping you from using the other four steps and keeping you from solving your problems. AND, TRY THE OTHER FOUR AGAIN.

You continue to be an excellent student as we knew you would be. You are brave, energetic, and creative. Keep using this process of *unpacking a problem,* taking one problem at a time. Keep it simple.

And do it again. And again. Make notes of what you discover each time about yourself and about your family. Good!

NOTES TO MYSELF

NOTES TO MYSELF

8 RESOURCES

And where do you go from here? If this process seemed to work well for you, go back to Chapter Three and begin again. This time select a different problem. Remember to remain flexible and creative as you do the steps of *unpacking*. You have begun to notice that you are winning some. You are feeling empowered and a bit more in charge! Congratulations.

However, if you're still having a problem with the process you might look again at the Chapter 4 about **maintainers**. What are you doing to keep things from changing? And why? Look again at Roadblocks in Chapter 7.

You might also change your perspective by re-reading the whole book upside down or with your hand covering your left eye. You might have a close friend or your spouse read it with you to see if you can find out, with their help, why this isn't working for you.

Keep at it. Progress may be slow but things will improve for you and your family. Persevere. Continue to be the courageous person you are. Give yourself credit and applause for that.

Whether or not you have found this process helpful, you may want to investigate some other alternatives. There are numerous books and tapes available which you might find helpful. Look at Other Resources. There are individuals trained in family counseling in nearly every city. There are agencies in your community developed specifically to assist parents and kids. You probably know this. By the time parents pick up *Parent Survival Training* they have usually tried everything. (Once again, see the list of things parents tried in the Appendix.)

Nonetheless, the key to getting help is finding the community people or agencies that are most suited to your needs. The way to discover the best ones for you is to call or ask around. We find word of mouth to be the best resource!

We have included a chart for you to fill out to help you in your search for assistance. If you'd prefer not to give your name, call anonymously or give a fictitious name. Choose an agency which you feel best meets your needs. Keep the chart near the telephone for those emergency times. You may wish to update your chart regularly because the people and the services provided in the agencies are constantly changing.

Whenever you seek services of any kind, be sure to ask how much it costs and how payment is made. You don't want to get in the position of those parents who have spent literally thousands of dollars trying to find solutions to their children's problems. Ask also for references from people who have used the services of the agencies.

COMMUNITY AGENCIES

Jot down the names of contact people, the telephone numbers, where they are located, what services they offer, and the cost of the services.

Police: ______________________________

____

Probation: ______________________________

____

Juvenile Hall: ______________________________

____

Counseling Agency: ______________________________

____

Psychologist: ______________________________

____

Community Mental Health: ______________________________

____

Helpline/Crisis Telephone: ______________________________

____

Parent Support Group: ____________________

____

Alcoholics Anonymous: ____________________

____

Alanon: ____________________

____

School Counselor: ____________________

____

Planned Parenthood: ____________________

____

Church/Temple: ____________________

____

Runaway House/Teen Shelter: ____________________

____

Other: ____________________

____

Private Non-profit Agencies

If you live in a city of any size you will probably find several private non-profit agencies in your community. Go to visit them, but please don't be put off by the physical environment of some. Because they tend to be youth oriented, they may not have the newest furnishings nor the best kept grounds, but they can provide services that are not provided by public agencies. The kinds of agencies we're taking about have many generic names: community based organizations, drop-in centers, free clinics, runaway houses, youth centers, and so on. These organizations had their beginnings in the 60's and are differently oriented and structured than more traditional institutions although after 20 years they now have a tradition of their own.

1. Hotlines or helplines: a good place to begin. Many communities have a telephone service which you can call with any sort of problem and be directed to the people or agencies that can assist you. Usually the call you make here will be anonymous and you can receive information on a multitude of different services. In our community this service is called "Community Resource and Information Service" (CRIS).

   Some hotlines provide crisis intervention counseling over the telephone, good for times of crisis, but they will refer you elsewhere for long term assistance.

   Most of these kinds of services belong to larger national associations. So, if you can't locate such a service locally, call the national association number. (See list following.)

2. Runaway houses: often communities have centers where kids can go when the tension at home becomes unbearable and a

"time-out" is needed for both the parents and the kids. These shelters also serve as safe havens for runaways or pushed out children. There is a national network of these programs, funded by the federal government. Most have been operational for at least a dozen years so the staff people in the centers are usually well trained and understand the dynamics of family problems. They may appear to be advocates of your teenager and this may not please you. The idea is that the child is more vulnerable and less able to articulate his needs. The practical matter is that if the teenager perceives the counselor as being his advocate, the teenager is more likely to be cooperative and go along with solutions.

These agencies can offer an alternative place for the kids to stay overnight for up to two weeks. Here they are safe and cared for. Use the runaway house when or before the situation reaches crisis proportions.

3. Individual and family counseling agencies. Most of the youth agencies described above offer counseling on sight. Many are more oriented to crisis intervention so do not provide long term, on-going family counseling. If they do not provide this, however, they will be able to refer you to people and agencies who can offer that kind of counseling . A sliding scale is often used to assess fees, meaning, the agency will take into consideration the family income when charging you for it's services.

4. Long term residential treatment programs. In drastic cases, you may find yourself with a teenager who is really out of control. Often he or she has had brushes with the law or is caught up in a serious drug or alcohol problem. You may need to arrange for long term residential treatment, if the authorities do

not take the matter out of your hands and place the child in such a program.

The kind of program in this category might be connected to a hospital, it might be a boys ranch or a girls "school." In any case, unless you are very poor, even if the court places your child you will ultimately be responsible for all or part of the costs. And the costs can be exorbitant, $2,000 to $5,000 per month. And the child may stay many months. This is the way parents find themselves spending their life fortunes on solving their kids' problems. You can call your county probation department, they will have a list of these types of placements.

It is crucial when looking for a program of this type to visit the plant. Talk to as many staff members as you can. Find out what the program costs. Discover whether it is a non-profit agency or for-profit business. It is our bias that non-profit agencies are more sound because money goes back into the operation of the program, rather than into the entrepreneur's pockets. (We have listed some residential programs and schools under Other Resources. We have not visited all of these schools so cannot be responsible for the quality of the services they provide.)

Public Agencies

Most counties in the United States are charged with providing social services to its citizens. States fund some programs and the United States Government funds programs and provides services in some cases. Again, your local hotline should be able to direct you to the people you need to speak to. If not, your county or community mental health services should be able to direct you to the agency appropriate for your needs.

1. Community Mental Health Services. Agencies within county governments which direct and operate small mental health services located throughout the county. The services usually charge on a sliding scale, provide adequate counseling, and can provide some good advice about who else you need to see. If your child has a drug or alcohol problem this might be the place to start. Some counties provide special services which address only these problems.

2. Social Welfare and Social Security. Usually, this would be the agency in the county that would provide money for whatever services you might qualify for. They will also become involved in cases where the child needs protective custody because of abuse or other serious family dysfunction. This agency might also be responsible for children who, because of their own behavior become wards of the juvenile court. The Social Welfare Department would assign a caseworker to supervise the child when he or she is placed away from the parents in foster care, which is usually in a private home where the adults are licensed to care for court wards.

3. Schools. Junior High and High Schools around the country provide various services for their troubled students. Most have counselors who are academically oriented and are only able to refer to other services. Some schools have counseling services which offer substantive counseling by mental health professionals as well as peer counseling in which the students participate in assisting one another. Sometimes you will discover the problems you are having with your child are very related to school problems and you need to work closely with the people there to clear up the difficulties.

3. Probation Department. Many parents do not see the probation department as an agency that is helpful, rather, they believe it causes more problems than it solves. Since it's an arm of the justice system or juvenile court system parents try to avoid it because of the stereotype of getting involved with "the authorities."

   In fact, juvenile probation and juvenile court can be helpful to parents if approached for information or with problems they are equipped to handle. If you are seeking psychotherapy for your child, probation is not the agency of choice. If you are seeking people who can assist in controlling an otherwise out of control child, this is the agency you want.

   Most probation departments provide both informal and formal processes in resolving problems. "Formal" means the case is adjudicated in court. "Informal" means the case is handled in simpler office proceedings. Each can be beneficial in different ways. Therefore, don't shy away from using these authorities because of some preconceived notion. They have been helpful to many thousands of families across the country.

Emancipation of Minors

In California, in 1978, a law was passed that allowed young people to become legally responsible for their own affairs: emancipated. This course is also available in other states. For information contact the office of your county clerk or the National Center for Youth Law as listed in Other Resources. You will find more descriptive information about California's "Emancipation of Minors" law in the Appendix.

Parent Support Groups

One of the most helpful methods of assisting parents is the development of support groups. These groups need not be professionally run but find their strength and effectiveness in the peer support they provide. Parents meeting with each other every week or every other week for a few hours can be of great benefit to the participants.

To inquire about those in your community, call your local helpline or call a community based youth and family counseling center. Your school may have such groups or know who does. Some churches have parent groups, this is another place to inquire. If a parent support group does not exist in your community give some thought to beginning one. The *Toughlove* reference listed in Other Resources has an excellent chapter on parent support groups. You might even use this *Parent Survival Training* book as a basis for beginning your own group.

The above agencies and groups are merely a few of the things that could be considered as resources and alternatives. Look for your own. Again, use your creativity.

Other Resources

Agencies, telephone numbers, books, and tapes

National Network Runaway and Youth Services (NNRYS): (202)-488-0739

National Center for Youth Law: (415)-543-3307

National Runaway Hotline:
- Chicago 1-(800)-621-4000
- Houston 1-(800)-231-6946

Parents & Friends of Lesbians and Gays, Inc.: (213-472-8952) P.O. Box 24565, L.A., CA 90024 (They can put you in touch with groups in your area.)

California Coalition of Youth and Family Counselors (CCYFC): (916)-443-2711

California Runaway Hotline: 1-(800)-843-5200

Gordon. *Parent Effectiveness Training*. Wyden Books, 1976.

Arnold. *Helping Parents Help Their Children.* Brunner/Mazel, 1978.

Buntman and Saris. *How To Live With Your Teenager*. Birch Tree Press, 1979.

Efron and Rowe. *The Strategic Parenting Manual.* 1987.
J.S.S.T., P.O.Box 2484, Station A,
London, Ontario, Canada N6A 4G7

How To Talk So Kids Will Listen and *Siblings Without Rivalry:* Group Workshop Kits. (Contain materials and cassettes.)
Negotiation Institute, Inc.
(212) 986-5555,
230 Park Avenue, New York, N.Y. 10169

Toughlove (Agency and book)
(215) 348-7090,
David and Phyllis York,
P.O. Box 1069, Doylestown, PA 18901

Forrest. *How To Cope With a Teenage Drinker: New Alternatives and Hope for Parents and Families*. New York: Atheneum, 1983.

Kolodny, Bratter, Deep. *How To Survive Your Adolescent's Adolescence.* Little, Brown & Company, 1984.

The Drug Abuse Council. *The Facts About "Drug Abuse."* New York: The Free Press, 1980.

Nielson. *How To Motivate Adolescents: A Guide for Parents, Teachers, and Counselors.* New Jersey: Prentice-Hall, 1982.

(The January/February, 1988, issue of *Professional Counselor Magazine*, Vol.2, No. 4, has an in depth view of adolescent inpatient treatment programs all over the United States. The programs discussed are primarily geared to treating adolescent alcohol or drug addicts. You'll be surprised how many there are and the diversity of programs offered! If you're interested, write to the publisher at 12729 N.E. 20th, Suite 12, Bellevue, WA 98005.)

A FEW ADOLESCENT INPATIENT TREATMENT PROGRAMS:

Provo Canyon School: A Charter Facility
(801) 227-2088
P.O. Box 1441, 4501 N. University Ave., Provo, Utah 84603

The Devereaux Foundation (residential school in 11 states.)
1-(800)-345-1292 x 3045 (outside Pennsylvania)
(215)-964-3045 (in Pennsylvania)
Box 400, 19 South Waterloo Road, Devon, PA 19333

The Oaks Treatment Center
1-800-THE-OAKS
1407 West Stassney Lane, Austin, TX 78745

COMMENTS FROM PARENTS

The following comments were made by parents two months after completing the PST Workshop using this book. We feel the best way to end is to let the parents speak for themselves.

"Parents need support. Parents need to talk and get together. Parents are being abused (horribly, sometimes) in this day and age of the child. I sat and listened to the incredible anger and hurt these people were going through, and felt compassion for them. Thank God for friends and classes to get you through! We all need hope. This book will give us a 'handbook of hope.' Hopefully parents can utilize this to its fullest."

"Most teenagers are a pain in the ass, but parents can survive it."

"I took small steps in understanding but the problems are as acute as ever. Thank you for your help."

"Things seem much improved. I still have trouble with her coming home on time, but she hasn't gotten into trouble."

"I can't stand the adolescent stage. I hate it!"

"The classes were a big help. Learning my kids were not too different from other people's kids and getting new ideas on how to cope was encouraging."

"Keeping calm helps!"

"I feel that with counseling and these workshops, things are much better. The main thing was seeing our problem in perspective. Thank you."

"Things have changed for the better, much due to our classs, and in part because he has matured some too. His grades are far better and he hasn't stolen from me."

Thanks again to all the parents who shared their lives with us and helped make this book a reality for the use of other parents in need.

APPENDIX

Worksheet	108
Unpacking Problems Chart	109
Traits of Families with Delinquent Youth	111
Methods of Dealing with Problems	112
Old Woman/Young Woman	113
Giving Up Losing Battles	114
A Vicious Circle	115
Maintainers	116
Myths	117
Monkey Wrenches	118
Roadblocks to Monkey Wrenches	120
Ways to Overcome Roadblocks	121
Emancipation of Minors (California)	122

WORKSHEET

1. What was the problem?

___

2. What were the possible **maintainers** of the problem? (What have you tried?)

___

3. What did you, the parent, want? (***minimum goal***)

___

What did the child want? (***minimum goal***)

___

4. What Monkey Wrenches were tried? (**Strategies**)

___

What worked?

___

5. General outcome? Comments.

___

Cut out and post in your house.

UNPACKING PROBLEMS

Questions to ask yourself when you're stuck!

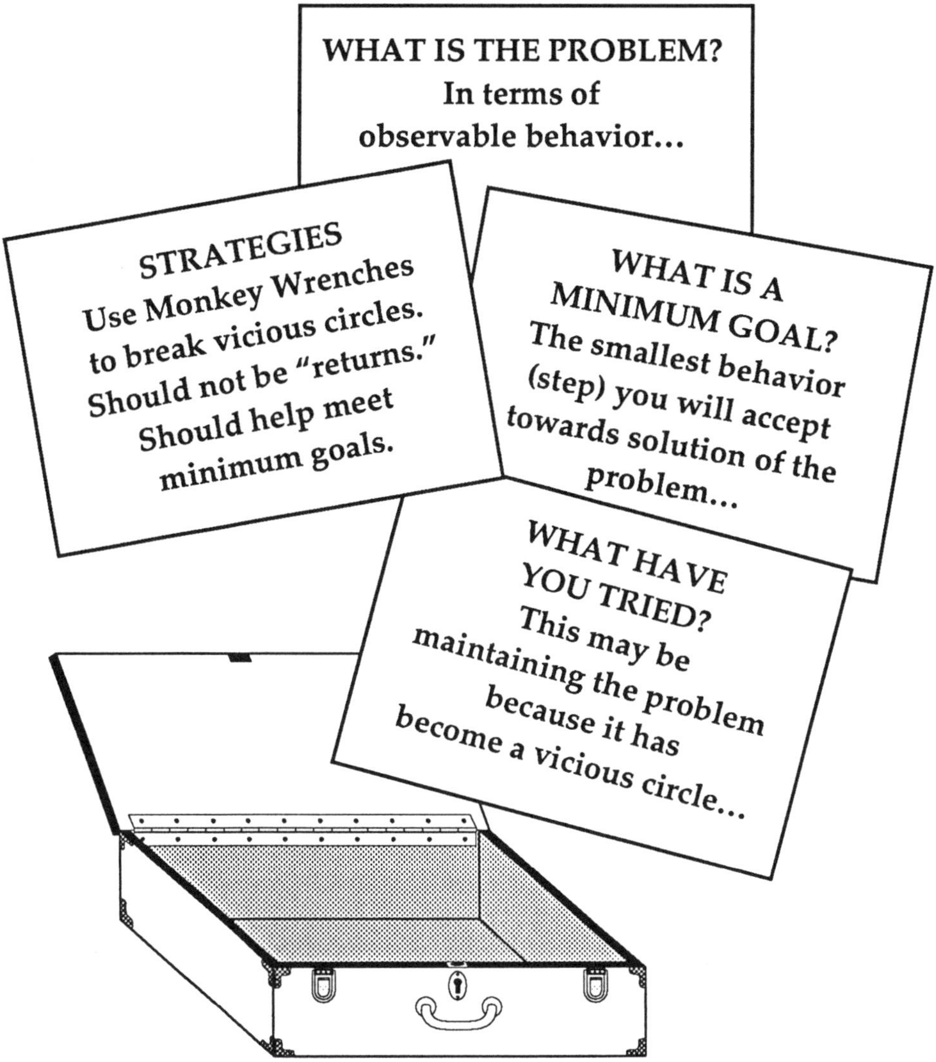

TRAITS OF FAMILIES OF DELINQUENT YOUTH

Research literature shows that families of delinquent youth have these traits when compared with families of non-delinquent youth. These are not listed in any prioritized way.

1. Fewer family activities.
2. Parents are less involved with children's activities.
3. Parents give less support to children. For example these parents fail to praise good behavior.
4. Less equality in family communication. For example the mother talks more than others.
5. Few positive interruptions. For example the parents fail to say,"That's good," or "I like that."
6. Less positive family interaction. Just being and talking together.
7. Less give and take among family members.
8. Communication within family is often not clear.
9. Lots of defensive communication. For example the parent insists he/she is right all the time.
10. Greater difference between how family really is and how [they believe] it should be.
11. More silence.
12. More rules.
13. "Hit and miss" with use of punishment when rules are broken.
14. Parents punish harder.
15. Father and mother differ more in how they see their family.
16. Parents see family as not meeting their needs.
17. Parents see family as harder to control.
18. Less orderly living schedule.
19. Less parenting education.
20. Less use of contracts to reach family goals.

METHODS OF DEALING WITH PROBLEMS

These methods were reported by parents in workshops as things that were tried but were unsuccessful. (Listed in order of popularity.)

1. **TALK**
   - Explain
   - Command
   - Lecture
   - Provide information
   - Logic
   - Yelling
   - Nagging
   - Family meetings
   - Common sense
   - Praise

2. **COUNSELING**
   - Drug & alcohol counseling
   - Klein Bottle (Youth Counseling Program)
   - Family doctor
   - Psychiatrist
   - Use friends
   - Visual charts

3. **TAKE AWAY THINGS**
   - Stereo, TV, food
   - Restrictions
   - Grounding
   - Bargaining
   - Church

4. **THREATS**

5. **SET RULES**
   - Chores
   - Make deadlines
   - Give more responsibility and chores
   - Send kid away
   - Wait it out
   - Humor
   - Give up
   - Role reversal
   - Separate eating places
   - Pull up marijuana plants

6. **MISCELLANEOUS**
   - Crying
   - Bribe
   - Love
   - Set example
   - Arrange work
   - Other activities
   - Punishments
   - Trade kids
   - Establish set of values
   - Make compromise
   - Be available
   - Give multiple choices
   - Juvenile Hall
   - Police
   - Ignore
   - Anger
   - Depression
   - Silence
   - Wipe slate clean
   - Pray
   - Share feelings
   - Trust
   - Listening
   - Parents separate
   - Pour water on kid

OLD WOMAN/YOUNG WOMAN

For those who had difficulty finding the two women...

The top picture is the same as the larger one in the text. It combines both the old woman and the young woman.

The middle picture has some of the features removed in order to more clearly show the old woman (approximately 80 years old).

In the bottom picture, some features have been removed and some added in order to more clearly show the young woman (approximately 25 years old) with her head turned away, looking back.

GIVING UP LOSING BATTLES

Some brief examples of what happened for some parents when thay gave up "losing battles."

1. I gave up yelling at my son to take a shower. I went a whole week and didn't say anything. I even took him to public places with me. After a week, he took a shower. GREAT!

2. I decided to stop nagging at my daughter about feeding the dog. I decided it would be my job, not hers. Well, she still doesn't feed the dog, but I sure feel better. It's one area we don't fight about anymore and things are a lot more pleasant when it's time for the dog to be fed.

3. I gave up on my daughter leaving her dirty clothes in the bathroom. I went for a week and now the dirty clothes have stretched out down the hall into the living room! I'm going to have to try something different.

4. We gave up the "come to dinner" battle by not setting a place for him anymore . Suddenly it was, "Where is my place? Don't I get any dinner?"

A VICIOUS CIRCLE

MOM: John, I would like to talk to you. Sit down, please. Have you been smoking marijuana again?

SON: (Looking at the floor) Oh, Mom, not this *again*.

MOM Now, don't lie to me. I found three of those funny cigarettes in your room yesterday, so don't even try to...

SON What! You were in my room? What gives you the right to snoop around in my dresser? Can't a person have any privacy around here?

MOM: I am your mother. This is my house and I will not put up with my son using drugs. Besides, if you expect me to wash your clothes for you and clean up after you, then I will continue to be in your room.

SON: Fine. Then I'll do my own wash. I didn't ask you to do it for me. I can take care of my own things and then maybe you'll stop getting on my case about everything all the time.

MOM: I'm not on your case "all the time." It's just that I love you and want you to learn to be responsible for yourself and learn how to live like a responsible person.

SON: Oh, *geez!* Here we go **again**! Just let me alone and I'll be fine.

MOM: Don't get smart with me, young man. Your attitude is something else I would like to speak to you about. As long as you intend to live in this house, you will not speak to your father and me in that tone of voice. We are your parents.

(And what happened to the drug problem?)

MAINTAINERS

This is a list that was generated by parents in PST workshops.

1. Always being right.
2. Always being logical and reasonable.
3. Having the last word.
4. Nagging.
5. Asking questions we know the answers to.
6. Threats.
7. Keep talking.
8. Yes, but....
9. Getting argumentative.
10. Questions that maintain.
11. Punishment upon punishment upon punishment.
12. Allowing the kid to manipulate the discussion, moving off of the real issue.

MYTHS

This is a list of some myths about parenting which we compiled at the workshops. Many parents felt these ideas helped **maintain** problems.

1. Broken homes cause delinquency.
2. Enough love will solve the problem.
3. Girls are less trouble than boys.
4. Parents are responsible for the behavior of their kids.
5. If kids are bad, the parents were bad.
6. If you're not in school activities, you won't do well in school.
7. Kids who get good grades don't get into trouble.
8. Hanging around with the right friends will keep kids from getting into trouble.
9. Alcohol is not as bad as dope.
10. If you do all the "normal" things (zoo, picnics, ball, etc.) your children will be good.
11. If you don't do what you are told, you won't amount to anything.
12. Educated adults make the best parents.
13. If it was good enough for me, then it's good enough for you.
14. Good parents meet all their kids needs.
15. Single parenting is always more difficult.
16. Good parents never yell.
17. Good parents are always rational.
18. You can't teach an old parent new tricks.

MONKEY WRENCHES

This is a list of some Monkey Wrenches with brief explanations. These were used by parent participants of PST.

1. Change the subject — in the middle of the heated argument start talking about something totally unrelated.

2. Silence — especially effective in arguments that are escalating. It's very difficult to have much of an argument when one person is silent.

3. Be "Up Front" — another way of saying honest. Be brutally honest with what you feel and see happening.

4. Give in — stops vicious circles dead when in the middle you say something like, "Well, I guess you're right. Okay."

5. Walk away — if you're angry or upset, it may be best to leave it for now and come back later. Walking away is very effective in combination with other Monkey Wrenches, such as, giving in, then walking away, or touch, then walking away.

6. Go to the extreme — take it to the limit. Exaggerate. One father had trouble with his daughter's messy room. He went in and really messed it up, throwing things around, etc. His daughter came home and said, "Who messed up my room?" He just laughed. And she cleaned her room.

7. Compromise — negotiations and contracts. "I'll do this if you do this." The mutually agreed upon contract can build in appropriate rewards and punishments.

8. Humor — great argument breakers. If joke telling isn't your style, try sticking pencils in your ears.

9. Touch — a very effective Monkey Wrench. Touch your children. For some, touch lightly, then walk away before the child has a chance to pull away and reject the touch.

10. "I feel...." — These are statements of how you are feeling about the behavior. The focus is on "I feel..." rather than "You did...." Examples: "I feel hurt." "I feel angry." "I feel used."

11. Paradox — saying the opposite of what you want. Contradictory statements. Example: "I want you to be late coming home every night this week." " I want you to turn up the stereo really loud and go sit next to it." "I think maybe it's time you quit school." "You can either take out the garbage or milk all the cows in the barn." (When you don't own cows or a barn.)

12. Do what you're accused of — your kid says, "You never listen to me." The Monkey Wrench is — don't listen.

13. Change Place — one parent in the midst of an argument took her kid into the shower. They both laughed so hard they couldn't fight. Or go for a ride in the car (captive audience) or go out to dinner or take a walk.

14. Do something outrageous — anything that stops the argument. Some examples: 1.) One parent picked up the kid's wet towels and put them on the kid's pillow then left for work. 2.) Another parent put garbage cans in the son's room where he couldn't miss them. 3.) Another parent threw a tangerine down hard on the kitchen floor, it squished all over, but made a definite impact on the kids and got them to stop fighting.

ROADBLOCKS TO MONKEY WRENCHES

This is a list of some of the things the parents felt kept them from trying new methods!

1. Fear of failing.
2. Fear of looking silly.
3. Inability to think of one.
4. Getting caught up in the vicious circle.
5. Enjoying the vicious circle.
6. Feeling uncomfortable acting out of character.
7. Not knowing when — timing.
8. Habit.
9. Humiliation.
10. Doubt it will work.
11. Fear of the unknown, what would follow.
12. Don't want to get down to their level.
13. "I've tried everything already."
14. Set goals too high.
15. "They should do as I ask without my having to do this."

WAYS TO OVERCOME ROADBLOCKS

This is a list of ideas parents used to overcome their Roadblocks.

1. Not lose my temper.

2. Let go a little — allow my kid some independence.

3. Combine forces with my spouse.

4. I might as well try, I haven't much to lose.

5. I need to learn to compromise and not want to win all the time.

6. It's more okay if I *choose* to be silly rather than having my kid always make me feel that way.

7. I'll just try harder.

8. Not interfere with my spouse when he has a plan.

9. I guess I need to let the kids make their own mistakes and let them suffer the consequences.

EMANCIPATION OF MINORS (CALIFORNIA)

In California, the Emancipation of Minors Act was passed in 1978 and enacted in 1979. According to the Act, any person under the age of 18 years who comes within the following description is an emancipated minor:

a.) Who has entered into a valid marriage, whether or not such marriage was terminated by dissolution; or
b.) Who is on active duty with any of the armed forces of the United States of America; or
c.) Who has received a declaration of emancipation pursuant to Section 64.

Section 64. Declaration of emancipation; petition; contents; notice; mandate.
a.) A minor may petition the superior court of the county in which he or she resides or is temporarily domiciled, for a declaration of emancipation. The petition shall be verified and shall set forth with specificity all of the following facts:

1.) That he or she is at least 14 years of age.

2.) That he or she willingly lives separate and apart from his or her parents or legal guardian with the consent or acquiescence of his or her parents or legal guardian.

3.) That he or she is managing his or her own financial affairs.

4.) That the source of his or her income is not derived from any activity declared to be a cime by the laws of the State of California or the laws of the United States.

b.) Before the petition is heard, such notice as the court deems reasonable must be given to the minor's parents, guardian, or other person entitled to the custody of the minor, or proof made to the court that their addresses are unknown, or that for other reasons such notice cannot be given. When a minor is a ward or dependent child of the court, notice shall be given to the probation department.

c.) The court shall sustain the petition if it finds that the minor is a person described by subdivision (a) and that emancipation would not be contrary to his or her best interests.

d.) If the petition is sustained, the court shall forthwith issue a declaration of emancipation, which shall be filed by the county clerk. Upon application of the emancipated minor, the Department of Motor Vehicles shall enter identifying information in its law enforcement computer network, and the fact of emancipation shall be stated on the department's identification cards issued to emancipated minors.

e.) If the petition is denied, the minor shall have a right to file a petition for a writ of mandate.

f.) If the petition is sustained, the parents or guardian shall have a right to file a petition for writ of mandate if they have appeared in the proceeding and opposed the granting of the petition.

g.) A declaration shall be conclusive evidence that the minor is emancipated.

INDEX

A

alcohol, 31, 56, 98, 100, 104, 112, 117
anger, angry, 16, 54, 69, 88, 105, 112

B

bargaining, 112
boys' ranch, 99
bribe, 15, 112
broken homes, 117

C

character, 121
child abuse, 100
communication, 14, 15, 16, 17, 31, 111
compromise, 72, 112, 119
contracts, 73, 111, 119
counseling, 15, 29, 94, 95, 98, 100, 103, 106, 112
counselors, 66, 67, 97, 98, 100, 103, 104
court ward, 100, 124
court, 99, 100, 124
crisis intervention, 98
custody, 124

D

deadlines, 12, 112
declaration of emancipation, 123
delinquency, delinquent, 14, 56, 111, 117
depression, 112
doctor, 112
dope, 56, 117
drinker, 103
drugs, 11, 14, 31, 37, 98, 100, 104, 112, 115
dysfunction, 100

E

emancipation, 101, 122, 123

F

family meeting, 35, 112
fear, 121
foster care, 100
friends, 14, 31, 43, 112, 117

G

gays, 103
goals, 63, 64, 65, 66, 69, 71, 111, 121
grades, 56, 66, 67, 110, 117
grounding, 112
groups, 96, 102, 103
guardian, 123, 124

H

habit, 121
honesty, 72, 119
hospital, 99
hotlines/helplines, 97, 99, 102, 104
humiliation, 121
humor, 18, 73, 112, 120

I

interventions, 71, 97, 98

J

juvenile court, 100, 101
juvenile hall, 95, 112

L

lesbians, 103
logic, logical, 112, 116
losing battles, 114
love, 87, 88, 112, 115, 117
lying, 31

M

mandate, 123
marijuana, 12, 112, 115
mental health, 96, 99, 100
minor, 123, 124
myths, 55, 56, 57, 84, 117

N

nag, nagging, 15, 16, 39, 53, 112, 114, 116
normal, 117

P

paradox, 73, 120
peer counseling, 102, 103
petition, 123, 124
physical violence, 15
police, 112
positive, 111
praise, 111, 112
private non-profit, 98
probation department, 95, 101, 102, 124
protective custody, 100
psychiatrist, 112
psychologist, 96
psychotherapy, 101
punish, punishment, 31, 111, 112, 116, 119

R

residential treatment programs, 98, 99, 100, 104
respect, respectfulness, 14, 29, 31, 38
restrictions, 15, 66, 112
rewards, 119
role-play, 21, 23, 25, 58, 67, 76
rules, 111, 112
runaways, viii, 14, 97, 98, 99, 102, 103

S

school activities, 117
school, 11, 12, 31, 44, 65, 66, 67, 97, 98, 99, 100, 103, 105, 117
shelter, 98, 99
single parenting, 118
Social Security, 100
social welfare, 100
spouse, 122
strategies, viii, 14, 15, 69, 71, 75, 77, 84, 88, 103

T

threats, 116
timing, 15, 54, 121
touch, 73, 120
Toughlove, 102, 103

U

unpacking, viii, 11, 13, 25, 38, 47, 51, 60, 63, 67, 69, 71, 75, 77, 88, 89, 93
"up front", 119

THE AUTHORS

Paul A. Smyth and Janet Benner, Ph.D.s, together founded a residential treatment program for youthful drug and alcohol abusers. For 20 years they have worked with runaways, delinquents, drop-outs, drug and alcohol abusers, and families in crisis with their troubled teenagers.

Dr. Smyth has a doctoral degree in psychology. He designed and directed seminars known as Parent Survival Training which taught thousands of parents how to deal with their recalcitrant youngsters. His own turbulent youth, in juvenile halls and jail, gave him a special insight in his work with parents. He consults with youth projects throughout the country.

Dr. Benner has a doctoral degree in Human Services Administration. Besides her work with teens, she directed a battered women's shelter, helped people in stop smoking and weight control programs. Her other books include *Smoking Cigarettes: The Unfiltered Truth.*

Tim Putz Photography

Rebecca Jeske, photographer

ORDER ADDITIONAL COPIES OF

PARENT SURVIVAL TRAINING:
A Guide to Parents of Teenagers ISBN 0-942723-13-9 $ 8.95

SMOKING CIGARETTES:
The Unfiltered Truth ISBN 0-942723-12-0 $ 10.95

Please send me _______copies of ______________________________
to the address below. Total payment in the amount of $_______* is enclosed.
*California residents please include 6% sales tax. The publisher will pay for shipping and handling. Please discount 40% for orders of three or more copies.

Name ____

Address ____

City ______________________________________ State ______ Zip ________

Make checks payable and mail to:

JOELLE PUBLISHING, INC.
P. O. Box 91229
Santa Barbara, CA 93190-1229